"Le Tombeau de Couperin"
and Other Works for Solo Piano

Maurice Ravel

DOVER PUBLICATIONS, INC.
Mineola, New York

Ravel's original orchestrations of *Ma Mère l'Oye, Valses nobles et sentimentales, Rapsodie Espagnole* and *Pavane pour une infante défunte* are published in *Maurice Ravel, Four Orchestral Works in Full Score,* (Dover, 1989: 0-486-25962-5).

Bibliographical Note

This Dover edition, first published in 1997, is a new compilation of previously uncollected piano works originally published separately. A. Durand & Cie, Paris, originally published: *Ma Mère l'Oye: 5 Pièces Enfantines,* 1910; *Valses nobles et sentimentales,* 1911; *Prélude,* 1913; *Le Tombeau de Couperin: Suite pour le Piano,* 1918; and *La Valse: Poème chorégraphique,* 1920. Editions Salabert, Paris, originally published: *À la manière de . . . Emmanuel Chabrier* and *À la manière de . . . Borodine,* both in 1914.

The Dover edition adds a composite list of contents in French and English, a glossary and background notes throughout. Ronald Herder translated the French terms and texts, and prepared the notes, based in part on Arbie Orenstein's *Ravel: Man and Musician,* (Dover, 1991: 0-486-26633-8).

International Standard Book Number: 0-486-29806-X

Manufactured in the United States of America
Dover Publications, Inc., 31 East 2nd Street, Mineola, N.Y. 11501

Contents

GLOSSARY OF FRENCH TERMS AND TEXTS

accélerez = accelerando
Alt(os), * violas
animez peu à peu, livelier little by little
arpéger le moins possible, arpeggiate as little as possible
assez animé, rather lively
assez lent—avec une expression intense, rather slow—with intensity
assez lent et très expressif (d'un rythme libre), rather slow and very expressive
   (rhythmically free)
assez vif, rather quick
augmentez [en augmentant] peu à peu = crescendo poco a poco
au mouv^t (un peu plus lent et rubato), in tempo (a bit slower and *rubato*)
avec charme, charmingly

B^ons [bassons], bassoons

C.Ang. [cor anglais], English horn
C.B. [contrebasses], string basses
cédez (très peu)(á peine) = ritardando (very little)(slightly)
Clar. [clarinette], clarinet
(3) cordes, literally, "three strings"—a cancellation of a previous
   "soft" pedal marking
Cors, French horns

doux et expressif, gentle and expressive

encore plus lent, still slower
en dehors (et expressif), prominent (and expressive)
en se perdant, dying away
environ, approximate, *circa*
expressif (et en dehors), expressive (and prominent)

Fl(ûte), flute

Harpe, harp
H^tb [hautbois], oboe

languissant, languid
la partie supérieure en dehors, bring out the upper line
le chant très en dehors, bring out the melody
léger, light
lent (et grave), slow (and solemn)
les petites notes doivent etre frappées sur le temps, play the small notes
   on the beat

m.d. [main droit], right hand
m.g. [main gauche], left hand
mais expressif, but expressive

*Ravel's keyboard transcription of *La Valse* (p. 91) includes shorthand references to details of his orchestration
 of the work. These abbreviations specify instrument(s) in the original full score.

meme mouv^t un peu plus las, the same tempo [but] a bit more languid
modéré—très franc, moderate—very free
moins fort, not so loud
moins vif, less lively
(1er) mouv^t = Tempo (I), *a tempo*
mouv^t de marche, march tempo
mouv^t de valse (très modéré) (viennoise), waltz tempo (very moderate)
   (in Viennese style)
mouv^t du début, same tempo as at the beginning
musette, bagpipe
mystérieux, mysterious

plus, more
plus lent (et en retenant jusqu'à fin), slower (and held back until the end)
presque lent (dans un sentiment intime), almost slow (in an intimate manner)
pressez (jusqu'à la fin), rush, hurry (until the end)
pressez un peu, rush a little

Quatuor, quartet (orchestral strings)

ral(enti) = *rallentando*
ralentir beaucoup = *molto rallentando*
retenez [retenu] = *meno mosso*
revenez au (mouv^t) = return to (tempo) (= *a tempo*)

sans faire vibrer, without vibrato
sans nuances, without shadings
sans ralentir = *non rallentando*
sonore, sonorous
sourdine, mute ["soft" pedal]
soutenu = *sostenuto*

toujours plus f, always louder
très court, very short
très doux et un peu languissant, very gentle and a bit languid
très doux, le chant en dehors, very gentle, the melody brought out
très expressif (et en retenant), very expressive (and held back)
très fluide, very fluid
très lent, very slow
très lointain, very distant
très modéré, very moderate
Tromp(ettes), trumpets

une corde, one string (= "soft" pedal)
un peu, a little
un peu en dehors (et bien expressif), somewhat prominent
   (and quite expressive)
un peu moins vif, not quite so lively
un peu pesant, a bit weighty
un peu plus animé, somewhat livelier
un peu plus lent, somewhat slower
un peu plus modéré, a bit more moderate
un peu plus vif et en accélérant, somewhat livelier and moving ahead
un peu retenu, slightly held back

V^{elles} (violoncelles), cellos
vif, lively
V^{ons} (violons), violins

QUOTATIONS IN THE MUSIC

Page 4: **"Petit Poucet"**

"He believed he'd easily find his way because of the bread that he'd strewn all along his path; but he was very surprised to find not one single crumb: the birds had come and eaten everything."

Page 7: **"Laideronnette"**

"She disrobed and entered the bath. Toy mandarins of both sexes were reflected in the water, singing and playing instruments: some had lutes fashioned from a nut shell; some, viols made from an almond shell—for one must match an instrument to the size of its player."

Page 14: **"La Belle et la Bête"**

—"When I think of your good heart, you don't seem so ugly to me."
—"Oh! Lady, yes! I have a good heart, but I'm a monster."
—"There are certainly men more monstrous than you."
—"Had I the wit, I would compliment you to thank you, but I'm only a beast."

. . . .

—"Beauty, will you be my wife?"
—"No, Beast!"

. . . .

—"I die happy since I've had the pleasure to see you one more time."
—"No, my dear Beast, you won't die: you'll live to become my spouse!"
". . . The Beast disappeared and there at her feet was only a prince more handsome than Love itself, thanking her for having broken the spell cast over him."

Page 23: **"Valses nobles"**

". . . [I am convinced that my book best illustrates what I have sought in writing, which is nothing but] . . . the delightful and always novel pleasure of a useless occupation."

From Henri de Régnier's novel
Les Rencontres de Monsieur de Bréot (1904)

To Mimie and Jean Godebski

Ma Mère l'Oye
Cinq pièces enfantines
[Mother Goose: Five children's pieces]

(1908–10)

Ravel's *Ma Mère l'Oye*, his evocation of "the poetry of childhood," is a suite of children's pieces based on five fairy tales. The work was composed between 1908 and 1910 for piano four hands, for the pleasure of Mimie and Jean Godebski, children of Ravel's close and influential friends Ida and Cipa Godebski at whose country home the composer completed the music. Ravel had already dedicated his *Sonatine* (1903–5) to the parents.

The music was dedicated to the children when the work was published in 1910. That same year, Ravel's friend Jacques Charlot transcribed the suite for solo piano. In 1911, Ravel orchestrated the work for a children's ballet of his own scenario, adding interludes and new movements.

The stories "Sleeping Beauty in the wood" and "Little Tom Thumb" first appeared in Charles Perrault's (1628–1703) *Mother Goose Tales; or Stories of Olden Times*, a collection of eleven stories for children. "'Little Homely,' Empress of the toy mandarins" appeared in *Serpentin Vert*, a story collection by Marie-Catherine, Comtesse d'Aulnoy (1650–1705), a well-known literary rival of Perrault. The traditional version of "Beauty and the Beast" was written by Marie Leprince de Beaumont (1711–80), based on very old, largely anonymous tales. The source of "The wondrous garden" is uncertain.

All prefatory notes by Ronald Herder, based in part on Arbie Orenstein's *Ravel: Man and Musician*, (Dover, 1991: 0-486-26633-8).

I. Pavane de la Belle au bois dormant

[Pavane of Sleeping Beauty in the wood]

II. Petit Poucet

[Little Tom Thumb]

Il croyait trouver aisément son chemin par le moyen de son pain qu'il avait semé
partout où il avait passé; mais il fut bien surpris lorsqu'il ne put retrouver une
seule miette: les oiseaux étaient venus qui avaient tout mangé. (Ch. Perrault.)

III. Laideronnette, Impératrice des pagodes

["Little Homely," Empress of the toy mandarins]

Elle se déshabilla et se mit dans le bain. Aussitôt pagodes et pagodines se mi
chanter et à jouer des instruments : tels avaient des théorbes faits d'une coquil
noix ; tels avaient des violes faites d'une coquille d'amande ; car il fallait bien propor-
tionner les instruments à leur taille. (Mme d'Aulnoy : Serpentin Vert)

IV. Les entretiens de la Belle et de la Bête

[Conversations of Beauty and the Beast]

– « *Quand je pense à votre bon cœur, vous ne me paraissez pas si laid.* » – « *Oh! dame oui! j'ai le cœur bon, mais je suis un monstre.* » – « *Il y a bien des hommes qui sont plus monstres que vous.* » – « *Si j'avais de l'esprit je vous ferais un grand compliment pour vous remercier, mais je ne suis qu'une bête.*

....

..« *La Belle, voulez-vous être ma femme?* » – « *Non, la Bête!...* »

....

– « *Je meurs content puisque j'ai le plaisir de vous revoir encore une fois.* » – « *Non, ma chère Bête, vous ne mourrez pas: vous vivrez pour devenir mon époux!... La Bête avait disparu et elle ne vit plus à ses pieds qu'un prince plus beau que l'Amour qui la remerciait d'avoir fini son enchantement.* (Mme Leprince de Beaumont).

V. Le jardin féerique

[The wondrous garden]

arpéger le moins possible

To Louis Aubert

Valses nobles
et sentimentales

[Elegant and lyrical waltzes]

(1911)

The adjectives "noble" and "sentimentale"—distinguishing between elegant and lyrical types of waltzes—is a distinction thought to have originated with Franz Schubert's publishers in his thirty-four *Valses sentimentales*, Op. 50 (1823), and ten *Valses nobles*, Op. 77 (ca. 1827), both works for solo piano.

Ravel's set of eight uninterrupted waltzes for piano, composed in 1911, is an homage to the Schubert models, with their lilting rhythms, rubato, balanced phrases, straightforward form and unexpected harmonic subtleties. "The title *Valses nobles et sentimentales* sufficiently indicates my intention of writing a series of waltzes in imitation of Schubert . . . The seventh waltz seems to me to be the most characteristic."*

Ravel orchestrated the work in 1912 to serve as music for the ballet *Adélaïde, ou le langage des fleurs* (Adelaide, or the language of flowers).

*from Ravel's "Autobiographical Sketch"

« . . . le plaisir délicieux
« et toujours nouveau d'une
« occupation inutile. »

(Henri de Régnier)

I

III

Modéré

IV

Assez animé ♩. = 80

VII

VIII

ÉPILOGUE
Lent ♩ = 76

pp expressif et en dehors.

p

pp

sourdine

3 cordes

p

m.d.

m.g.

mp

pp

(♮)

sourdine

3 cordes

mf très expressif

m.d.

m.g.

pp

p

THREE SHORT PIECES
(1913)

Prélude

À la manière de . . . Emmanuel Chabrier
Paraphrase sur un air de Gounod
[In the style of Emmanuel Chabrier—Paraphrase on a melody by Gounod]

À la manière de . . . Borodine
(Valse)
[In the style of (Alexander) Borodin—Waltz]

To Mademoiselle Jeanne Leleu

Prélude

(1913)

À la manière de . . . Emmanuel Chabrier

Paraphrase sur un air de Gounod ("Faust IIème acte")

[*In the style of Emmanuel Chabrier—Paraphrase on a melody by Gounod**]

(1913)

*Siebel's flower song, "Faites-lui mes aveux"—labeled "Faust, Act II"—appears in Act III, Scene 1, of authoritative editions.

À la manière de . . . Emmanuel Chabrier   53

À la manière de . . . Borodine

(Valse)

[In the style of (Alexander) Borodin—Waltz]

(1913)

Le tombeau de Couperin

Suite pour le Piano

[Couperin's tomb: Suite for piano]

(1914–17)

Formal compositions by his pupils honoring a departed master grew out of an ancient historical tradition. In Europe of the 14th to 17th centuries, such works were labeled *apothéose* (glorification), *plainte* or *déploration* (lamentation), or *tombeau* (literally, a tomb—a monument to the dead). Ockeghem wrote one for Binchois . . . Josquin for Ockeghem . . . Gombert for Josquin. Influenced by the music of Corelli, Couperin acknowledged his musical debt in his "Grande Sonate en Trio" entitled *Le Parnasse ou l'apothéose de Corelli.*

Ravel, however, explained that his *Le tombeau de Couperin* was an homage to eighteenth-century French music rather than a personal tribute to François Couperin (1668–1733), called *"le Grand."* Nevertheless, he prepared for the task at hand by transcribing a suitable model: a forlane from Couperin's chamber work *Concert royaux.*

Ravel composed his suite of piano pieces between 1914 and 1917, then orchestrated it in 1919, omitting the fugue and toccata. Despite the elegaic mood of the fugue and his own forlane—considered the outstanding achievement of the suite—the original piano set is essentially a return to eighteenth-century clarity and elegance, recalling the spare textures, rapid ornamentation, perpetual motion and brilliant virtuosity of the harpsichord works of Rameau, Couperin and Domenico Scarlatti—innovations said to have influenced the keyboard works of Johann Sebastian Bach.

The six movements are dedicated to the memory of close friends who died in World War I.

To the memory of Lieutenant Jacques Charlot

I. Prélude

II. Fugue

Le tombeau de Couperin

To the memory of Lieutenant Gabriel Deluc

III. Forlane

To the memory of Pierre and Pascal Gaudin

IV. Rigaudon

To the memory of Jean Dreyfus

V. Menuet

To the memory of Captain Joseph de Marliave

VI. Toccata

To Misia Sert

La Valse

Poème chorégraphique

[The Waltz: Choreographic poem for orchestra]

(1919–20)

Transcribed by the composer

La Valse: Poème chorégraphique gestated in Ravel's mind for fourteen years. In a letter written in early 1906, he spoke of plans to write a waltz that would be a sort of homage to Johann Strauss: "You know of my deep sympathy for these wonderful rhythms, and that I value the *joie de vivre* expressed by the dance . . ." By 1914 the work had evolved into *Wien: Poème symphonique* (Vienna: symphonic poem)—described by Ravel as "a sort of apotheosis of the Viennese waltz," intermingled with "the impression of a fantastic and fatal whirling":

> "Through whirling clouds" (the composer wrote in a program note to the original publication), "waltzing couples may be faintly distinguished. The clouds gradually scatter: one sees at letter A [p. 95, m. 4], an immense hall peopled with a whirling crowd. The scene is gradually illuminated. The light of the chandeliers bursts forth at the fortissimo at letter B [p. 97, m. 7]. An imperial court, about 1855."

An intriguing possibility of a link between Ravel and Edgar Allen Poe has been suggested by some—specifically, a connection between Ravel's "fantastic and fatal whirling" and the "masked ball of the most unusual magnificence . . . a gay and magnificent revel . . . [that] went whirlingly on" in Poe's short story "The Masque of the Red Death" (1842). Scholars acknowledge Poe's role in French literature as that of a "poetic master-model," and that the French Symbolists borrowed freely from his imagery.

Ravel dedicated *La Valse: Poème chorégraphique*—its definitive title—to his long-time friend, the influential Misia Sert (*née* Godebski), sister of his close friend Cipa Godebski [see our note to *Ma Mère l'Oye*, p. 2]. This remarkable woman was highly esteemed by Mallarmé, and her portrait was painted by Renoir; her salons continually attracted the most talked-about personalities of the day. It was in her home, in the spring of 1920, that Ravel first performed a two-piano version of the work for Ballets Russes impresario Serge Diaghilev, choreographer Léonide Massine and composers Igor Stravinsky and Francis Poulenc.

Ravel's transcription for solo piano incorporates occasional small-note excerpts of orchestral elements from the full score. Since these are generally impractical or impossible to play along with the principal music, the player should regard those elements as references only, to frame or give dimension to what is already there to perform.

Mouv^t de Valse viennoise